THE LANGUAGE THEATER

A FUN, FULLY ILLUSTRATED GRAMMAR BOOK

Written by Maria Beatty
Illustrated by Bill Skrief
Edited by Glenn Beatty

www.TheLanguageTheater.com

ISBN: 978-1-54399-896-2

From the Author:

It is often asked of an author, "Why did you write this book?"

Grammar is the key to good communication
and the better the communication, the better the world.
We start at the beginning, with children.

The Problem:
English Grammar is complex and supposedly "boring."

The Solution:
I was inspired by a Denis Diderot quote I learned as a child.
"Language is a theater. The words are the actors."

The Parts of speech are the wonderful actors in the "Language Play!" These distinct characters talk to us from the stage. Each "actor" tells us what they do and how they interact with one another. Each grammar rule is represented with a simple sentence and picture so it is readily understood. We all love pictures and learn from them.

Depending on the student's level of understanding, one can select individual pages or sections to serve the needs of very young children through middle school. The theatrical visuals also make this guide an excellent tool for students learning English as a second language.

Everything you need is here.

Bill, Glenn and I hope you have as much fun learning from
The Language Theater as we had creating it!

Take the stage!

Maria Beatty

"Language is a theater.
The words are the actors."
-Denis Diderot

The Language Theater is an appealing, imaginative textbook which uses captivating illustrations that simplify and clarify the foundations of English Grammar. Career teacher Maria Beatty's link between grammar and theater is created by making each part of speech an "actor" who enters The Language Theater and performs their specific grammatical function as they interact with the rest of the cast. Whether it's for young learners, adults looking for simple explanations, or ESL students who may have difficulty grasping the usual text-laden tome, The Language Theater provides a uniquely different approach that pairs English language insights with a lively theatrical interpretation that's easy to understand.

D. Donovan

Senior Reviewer,

Midwest Book Review

For My Parents
for their unconditional love for all children
and their unconditional love of learning

Special Thanks to:

Cybele Georgiades for being a role model of reason, clarity and care

Odette Boudouris for making learning fun

Glenn Beatty for his love, support and for making the book happen

Chrysanthos Petsilas for his love and support

Bill Skrief for his genius, the amazing characters he created and his generous spirit

The Language Theater
makes learning English Grammar
easy and fun for everyone.

IF YOU ARE

A TEACHER...

This serves as a roadmap. Depending on the level and the ability of your students, you may make adjustments, provide focus, and add or subtract where needed. I have provided exercises at the end of each chapter, but I'm sure you will have ideas of your own.

A PARENT...

You have an engaging, straightforward, visual reference for most questions your child will ask about Grammar.

LEARNING ENGLISH AS A SECOND LANGUAGE...

Through simple pictures and short textual explanations, this book helps make learnging English Grammar easier and more enjoyable.

PLEASE SPREAD THE WORD!
Good reviews help.
Write a review on our website, TheLanguageTheater.com,
and on Amazon.

Table of Contents

~

Hello!
Welcome to the largest theater in the world,

The Language Theater!

I'm Theo the Grammarian,
the in-house director.

In the programs of this theater,
which is indeed the greatest of all...

...you'll find every story and every sentence
that has ever been spoken or written.

Its actors are an amazing group of performers who never get tired!

In this book they are going to speak to you about the roles they play. So, let's welcome the leader of this incredible group...

VERB

Hello! I'm VERB.

I appear in every single performance.
There is no sentence without me.
I'm also the only part of speech
that can create a sentence all by myself!

"Dance!"

I can be ACTIVE
when I do the action.

"I jumped over the fence."

I can be PASSIVE
when the action is
done to me.

"I was hit by
a snowball."

I can express a STATE of mind or being.

"I am."

I can express an EVENT.

"It is raining."

I can express a **FACT.***

"I **had** fish for lunch."

I can express a **FEELING.****

"He **feared** that spiders **were** in the closet."

I can express a **POSSIBILITY.****

"If I **won** the race I **would get** the prize."

*A **VERB** in the Indicative Mood expresses fact, opinion, assertion or asks a question.

A **VERB in the Subjunctive Mood expresses a condition that is doubtful or non-factual. It is used after "if" or a verb that expresses doubt, wish, regret, request, or demand.

I can
DOUBT.**

"We doubt he would be guilty."

I can
WISH.**

"I wish we would go to the museum this afternoon."

I can
GIVE ORDERS.***

"STOP!"

***A VERB in the Imperative Mood expresses a request or command.

Beware of me in the Subjunctive Mood!!!

In the Present Tense, I drop the "s" or "es" in the Third Person Singular.

" I wish she stays longer this time."

"We recommend that she rushes to catch the boat."

When I am the Verb "to be"...

...in the Present Tense,
I always wear
the "be" costume.

"The teacher asks that...

I be patient."

you be patient."

he/she be patient."

we be patient."

you be patient."

they be patient."

in the Past Tense,
I always wear
the "were" costume.

"I wish...

I were a better swimmer."

you were a better swimmer."

he/she were a better swimmer."

we were better swimmers."

you were better swimmers."

they were better swimmers."

I can also play the role of a NOUN, ADJECTIVE or ADVERB.

NOUN	ADJECTIVE	ADVERB

"Reading is fun."	"His camping tent is too small."	"She went to receive her prize dancing."

I can express an action...

In the PRESENT

"I play baseball every day."

In the PAST

"I played baseball yesterday."

In the FUTURE

"I will play baseball tomorrow."

I have eight helpers:

They are my auxiliary team.
In their various forms* they help me ask questions, say "yes" or "no" and be specific about the time and manner of an action.

They are all called **AUXILIARIES**!

Here is how they help!!!

"We are going to the movies."

"Do you like spinach?"

"We have never been to Alaska."

Here are a few more...

"Can you please be quiet?"

"We may sail today."

"You must leave!"

...and more!!!

"Shall I read this book?"

"Tom will come with us to the movies."

"I do not like sardines."

Sometimes the AUXILLARY VERBS "be, have, do and can" play my role in a sentence. They become the main VERB. Such as:

"I was at the library all day."

"My grandparents have a house in Vermont".

Now, please get paper & pencil so you can write down your answers!

VERB EXERCISE #1

Guess what my role is in each of the following sentences.

Choose the right answer:

1. Finish your work!
   a) order b) wish

2. I ran to school today.
   a) active b) passive

3. I earned an A+ on my test.
   a) fact b) possibility

4. It snowed last night.
   a) doubt b) event

5. This picture was drawn by my brother.
   a) active b) passive

6. She loves to wear her reading glasses.
   a) noun b) adjective

7. Interrupting is rude.
   a) noun b) adverb

8. The veterinarian recommends that my puppy take the medicine.
   a) indicative b) subjunctive

VERB EXERCISE #2

Draw a picture using an example from Exercise #1.

VERB EXERCISE #3

What do my auxiliaries (helpers) express in the following sentences?

1. Does he feel better?
   a) time b) manner c) question

2. They might leave tomorrow.
   a) say "no" b) time c) possibility

3. I will join you at the movies.
   a) time b) question c) purpose

4. Could you please help me find my glasses?
   a) question b) manner c) time

5. We must leave for the theater early.
   a) question b) manner c) necessity

6. We should allow enough time to get there.
   a) manner b) obligation c) time

VERB SUMMARY

I'm action itself!

I can be:
ACTIVE or PASSIVE.

I can:
express a FACT, FEELING, POSSIBLITY, DOUBT, WISH or GIVE ORDERS.

I can play the role of:
NOUN, ADJECTIVE or ADVERB.

I can express an action happening in the PRESENT, the PAST or the FUTURE.

I have eight helpers; they are my AUXILIARY team.

And now, let's all welcome our second magnificent actor...

NOUN

Hello! I'm NOUN.

Most of you know me as NAME
because this is what I do.
I name!

I'm in most performances.

I can be
the name of
a PERSON.

"Eve is pretty."

I can be
the name of
an ANIMAL.

"Our cat is fat."

I can be
the name of
a THING.

"I can't find
my pencil!"

I can be
the name of
a PLACE.

"He lives on
an island."

I can be the name of a QUALITY or an IDEA.

"This is a flower of great beauty!"

"He always speaks the truth."

I'm called DIMINUTIVE when I name something very small, young or dear.

"The kitten slept in my bed last night."

I'm called PROPER when I am a special name for a person, an animal, a thing or a place.

"Dylan loves to read!"

"Our dog, Lassie, loves to play with me."

As you can see, when I'm PROPER, my first letter is capitalized.

"Texas is a huge state."

I can also be the name of a JOB...

"Our teacher rides to school on his motorcycle."

...or I can be the name of a GROUP.

"Our neighbor has a bunch of dogs!"

I can name one thing...
SINGULAR

...or I can name many things.
PLURAL

"I saw a tiger at the circus."

"I saw three tigers at the zoo."

Sometimes, I look the same whether I'm SINGULAR or PLURAL.

"I saw a deer in the woods."

"I saw deer in the woods."

Sometimes,
I do the action,
so
I'm called the SUBJECT.

"Alex ate."

Sometimes,
I receive the action,
so
I'm called the OBJECT.

"She wrote a poem."

Very often, I play both the SUBJECT and the OBJECT in the same sentence.

"Bill painted a picture."

With an apostrophe (') and an "s"
or
just an apostrophe (') on my tail
I show possession.

"Laura's dress is beautiful!"

"The buses' windows are big."*

*When I end with an "s", singular or plural, the apostrophe always comes after me.

Now, please get paper & pencil so you can write down your answers!

NOUN EXERCISE #1

Guess whether I am the SUBJECT or the OBJECT in the sentences below.

		subject	or object
1.	I saw a giraffe.	☐	☐
2.	My father likes to drive fast.	☐	☐
3.	He loves ice cream.	☐	☐
4.	She wrote a beautiful poem.	☐	☐
5.	Her poem was better than mine.	☐	☐
6.	They sell flowers.	☐	☐
7.	The farmers work hard.	☐	☐
8.	My puppy is naughty.	☐	☐
9.	Melissa's hat is very pretty.	☐	☐

NOUN EXERCISE #2

Guess whether I'm SINGULAR (one) or PLURAL (many) in the following examples.

		singular	or	plural
1.	school	☐		☐
2.	notes	☐		☐
3.	boy	☐		☐
4.	forest	☐		☐
5.	dolphins	☐		☐
6.	book	☐		☐
7.	men	☐		☐
8.	bicycle	☐		☐
9.	sharks	☐		☐
10.	women	☐		☐
11.	flower	☐		☐
12.	sheep	☐		☐

NOUN EXERCISE #3

Can you run around the square below and draw a circle around ME every time you see ME?

large	remember	bear	yes	Italy	smart	apple
paper						more
gave						courage
horse						boat
heard						orchestra
eyes						but
never						in
kitchen						piglets
trees	height	violin	have	by	Yes!	Jason

NOUN SUMMARY

I'm present in most performances (sentences).

I can name a:
PERSON, ANIMAL, THING, PLACE, QUALITY or IDEA.

I can be PROPER (a special name).

I can name ONE (SINGULAR)...
or I can name MANY (PLURAL).

I can be the name of a GROUP.

I can be the name of a JOB.

I can perform the action (SUBJECT)...
or receive the action (OBJECT).

When I name something small, young or dear,
I'm called DIMINUTIVE.

And now, please, let's welcome our next wonderful actor...

ARTICLE

Hello! I'm ARTICLE.

I'm always where NOUN is.
I walk next to it. I hold its hand.

I'm also called the "pointer" because I point to the NOUN.

I'm called DEFINITE when I perform with a NOUN that points to a specific person, animal, thing, place, quality, attribute or condition.

"The babies are crying."

"The tree is very tall."

"The tension is thick."

I'm called INDEFINITE when I perform with a NOUN that points to any one person, place or thing.*

"She ate an apple."

"You're an hour late."*

"He is a hero."

"She is going to a university."

*I'm "AN" with a NOUN that starts with a vowel sound.
I'm "A" with a NOUN that begins with a consonant sound.

BUT...
I NEVER come on stage to point to any person, place or thing in the plural. NOUN doesn't need me for this play.
*Example: "You are hours late!"

When ADJECTIVE joins NOUN
I hold ADJECTIVE's hand.

"She is wearing
a beautiful bow."

"He is wearing
a stylish suit."

As you see, I can be DEFINITE or INDEFINITE.
I play these two roles again and again and again.

Now, please get paper & pencil so you can write down your answers!

ARTICLE EXERCISE #1

Am I DEFINITE or INDEFINITE?
Place me in the right box.
The first one is done for you.

	definite	or indefinite
1. The bus was crowded.	The	
2. We read an interesting book.		
3. I found a dollar on the street.		
4. They climbed up a hill!		
5. An honest person always speaks the truth.		
6. We saw a flamingo at the zoo.		

ARTICLE EXERCISE #2

Fill in the blanks in the paragraph below with the right form and role of ME.

Yesterday, I went to ______ zoo with my father. I saw ______ lion and his cubs, ______ hippopotamus, ______ elephant, many deer, many tigers and ______ chimpanzee. All ______ animals seemed well-cared for and happy.

ARTICLE EXERCISE #3

Draw a picture of ME in the box provided below, performing one of my roles in the story on the previous page.

ARTICLE SUMMARY

I'm always where NOUN is.

I can be either
DEFINITE or INDEFINITE.

And now, please, let's welcome our next exciting actor...

ADVERB

Hello! I'm ADVERB.

My name means "near the VERB,"
because most of the time I perform with VERB.
I help VERB show its meaning.

I can be an ADVERB of AFFIRMATION or YES!

"I really liked your gift."

I can be an ADVERB of NEGATION or NO!

"Forget me not."

I can be an ADVERB of DOUBT.

"Maybe my sister will let me use her makeup."

I can be an ADVERB of PLACE or LOCATION.

"There is a gas station nearby."

"The children are playing outside."

I can be an ADVERB of DIRECTION.
I can show where something comes from or goes to.

"He looked upwards."

I can be an ADVERB of CAUSE or REASON and answer the questions *why?* or *for what purpose?*

"He didn't come to school because he was sick."

I can be an ADVERB of DEGREE.
I can answer the questions *how much* or *how little*...

"She completely forgot our appointment."

I can be an ADVERB of MANNER
and answer the questions *how* or *in what way*.

"They danced beautifully."

I can be an ADVERB of TIME and answer the questions *when, at what time, how soon, how long, how often* and the like.

"We're going to Disneyland again soon."

I can be an ADVERB of NUMBER.

"He finished first."

When I ask questions like when, where, how, or why, I'm also called INTERROGATIVE.

"How did I do this?"

I'm called VERBAL when I'm glued to the meaning of the VERB.

"She's looking forward to watching her show."

"He gave up."

Sometimes I come on stage
holding the hand of an ADJECTIVE.

"Your car is
so cool."

Now, please get paper & pencil so you can write down your answers!

ADVERB EXERCISE #1

What does my name mean?

" ______________________________ "

ADVERB EXERCISE #2

Guess what kind of an ADVERB I am in the sentences below.

Circle the right answer:

1. I learn **best** when I get enough sleep.
   a) affirmation b) number c) degree

2. He doesn't make mistakes **when** he's focused.
   a) negation b) time c) purpose

3. The children are playing **upstairs**.
   a) time b) place c) doubt

4. We stepped in the puddle **therefore** our shoes got wet.
   a) reason b) time c) manner

5. She **never** answers the phone.
   a) reason b) negation c) manner

6. I covered the mess **up** and ran to school.
   a) interrogative b) manner c) verbal

7. **Why** are you complaining?
   a) verbal b) interrogative c) manner

ADVERB EXERCISE #3

Draw a picture related to one of the sentences on the previous page.

ADVERB
SUMMARY

My name means "near the VERB"
because most of the time I perform with VERB.

I can be an ADVERB that shows:
AFFIRMATION, NEGATION, DOUBT, REASON, PLACE, DIRECTION, TIME, MANNER, DEGREE OR NUMBER.

I can be:
INTERROGATIVE (ask questions)...
or VERBAL (glued to a verb).

I can perform with ADJECTIVE.

And now, please, let's welcome our next marvelous actor...

ADJECTIVE

Hello! I'm ADJECTIVE.

I always come on stage with either NOUN or PRONOUN.
I enhance their meanings.
How? By changing, qualifying or defining them.

I'm VERY flexible.
Some say I'm made of rubber.

Look at all of these SUFFIXES and PREFIXES I can put on...

renewable
festive
bluish
fortunate
thirsty
hilarious
fragile
coordinate
unhappy
choral
comical
silken
divine

restless
funny
verbose
irreplaceable
important
improper
grateful
western
vigorous
famous
quarrelsome
annoyed
resting

...and much, much more!!!

Most of the time,
I come on stage in front of NOUN.

"I'm wearing a
new pair of shoes."

Sometimes though, for grace and emphasis of expression
I follow the NOUN and then I'm called POETICAL
because I play this part a lot in poetry.

"The sky, bright and blue,
was clear of clouds."

I can be
QUALITATIVE.

"He's wearing a white hat."

I can be
QUANTITATIVE.

"I like the first hat on the left."

Sometimes, I'm called
PURE.

"Melissa wore her new glasses."

Sometimes, I'm called
DERIVED.

"Dylan is playing with his newborn brother."

Sometimes, I'm called PROPER because I come from a proper name.

"American hamburgers are the best."

I'm called PRONOMINAL when I come on stage
wearing PRONOUN's costume.

"This bicycle is a wreck."

"This" is a PRONOUN, but here we call it
a pronominal ADJECTIVE. Can you guess why?

I'm called SUBSTANTIVE when I replace NOUN and come on stage holding ARTICLE's hand.

"Only the well-behaved will get a cookie!"

To indicate more of a quality
I change my form by adding -ER or -EST.

"He is taller than me."

"She is the smartest girl in the class."

Also, to indicate more or less of a quality
I go on stage with one of these four ADVERBS:
MORE, LESS...

"I'm more tired than you."

"You're less tired than me."

...MOST or LEAST.

"He is the most powerful man on earth."

"I'm the least interested in watching this movie."

Now, please get paper & pencil so you can write down your answers!

ADJECTIVE EXERCISE #1

Underline the prefix or the suffix I am wearing in each of the words below.

BE CAREFUL!
Sometimes I wear both; a prefix and a suffix!

Thankful

Greenish

Effortless

Floral

Sailing

Cooperative

Courageous

Encouraged

Interactive

Extraordinary

Subordinate

Eastern

ADJECTIVE EXERCISE #2

Guess my role in the following sentences.

Circle the right answer:

---

1. I will go fly my new kite.
   a) proper b) derived c) pure

2. His Italian friend is very tall.
   a) proper b) poetical c) pure

3. My hard-won victory came with a big prize.
   a) pure b) derived c) substantive

4. This sailboat, so white, looks like a seagull.
   a) proper b) derived c) poetical

5. These toys are broken.
   a) pure b) pronominal c) substantive

6. The most studious won the prize.
   a) derived b) substantive c) pure

ADJECTIVE EXERCISE #3

Am I indicating MORE or LESS here?

		more	or	less
1.	She's the prettiest baby I have ever seen.	☐		☐
2.	He is more advanced in math than me.	☐		☐
3.	I am the least worried about it.	☐		☐
4.	We are most interested in ballet.	☐		☐
5.	Her skirt is longer than mine.	☐		☐
6.	You are less busy than me.	☐		☐

ADJECTIVE SUMMARY

I always come on stage with either NOUN or PRONOUN.

I can put on innumerable PREFIXES or SUFFIXES.
I'm very flexible!!!

I can be:
PURE, DERIVED, PROPER, POETICAL, QUALITATIVE, QUANTITATIVE, or PRONOMINAL.

When I come on stage replacing NOUN and holding ARTICLE's hand, I'm called SUBSTANTIVE.

I can indicate MORE...or I can indicate LESS.

And now, please, let's welcome our next incredible actor...

PRONOUN

Hello! I'm PRONOUN.

For simplicity and beauty,
I come on stage to replace NOUN.

"Glenn took his mother the book
she asked him to bring her."

For fun, let's see how tiring this play would be for NOUN and the audience if I didn't exist.

"Glenn took Glenn's mother the book Glenn's mother asked Glenn to bring Glenn's mother."

Sometimes, I play more than one role
in the same sentence.

"He, who wrote this poem, is a famous poet."*

*He is a personal pronoun. Who is a relative pronoun.
Wait a few pages and all will be made clear!

Sometimes I even replace a group of words that play the role of NOUN.

"To be, or not to be: that is the question."

At times I fill in for NOUN
because NOUN cannot be used.

"It is snowing."

*You don't want to say, "Snow is snowing." Right?

I can be PERSONAL.

"I told her everything about me and the farm."

I can be RELATIVE when I replace a NOUN, another PRONOUN or a group of words that come before me and I become the linking word in a sentence.

"This is the brush that I used to paint my car."

*Common RELATIVE PRONOUNS are who, whom, whose, which and that.

I can be POSSESSIVE.

"The blue car is mine."

I can be REFLEXIVE when I add the words 'self' or 'selves' to my tail for emphasis or clarification.

"I painted it myself."

I can be
INDEFINITE.

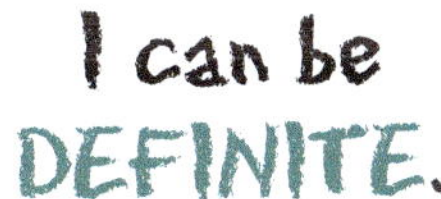

"Nobody came to my party."

"A party!!!
That is my favorite pastime."

*The Indefinite PROUNOUN doesn't refer to a specific person or thing.
The Definite PRONOUN does refer to a specific person or thing.
(Personal and Demonstrative PRONOUNS are also called Definite PRONOUNS)

I can be
INTERROGATIVE.

"Which of you did this?"

Or I can be
DEMONSTRATIVE.

"This is really yummy!
Shhh, don't tell anyone!"

I'm simple, gracious, and always beautiful!
(Do you think I have a big head about this?)

Now, please get paper & pencil so you can write down your answers!

PRONOUN EXERCISE #1 & 2

1. What does my name mean?

___

2. Underline me in the following sentences and then guess my role(s) in each.

    1. I love you.

    ___ ___

    2. Our teacher told us to be quiet.

    ___ ___

    3. The grammar book is mine.

    ___

    4. The poem that he wrote about friendship is beautiful.

    ___ ___

    5. His puppy barked at us.

    ___ ___

    6. Who do you think is stronger?

    ___ ___

    7. We painted our home ourselves.

    ___ ___ ___

PRONOUN SUMMARY

I come on stage replacing NOUN.

Sometimes I replace MYSELF!
(I play two characters in the same sentence.)

Sometimes I replace a group of words
that play the role of NOUN.

I can be:
PERSONAL, RELATIVE,
POSSESSIVE, REFLEXIVE,
DEFINITE, INDEFINITE,
INTERROGATIVE or DEMONSTRATIVE.

And now, please, let's welcome our next incredible actor...

CONJUNCTION

Hello! I'm CONJUNCTION.

They call me "The Great Matchmaker" because I connect words, phrases, clauses or even sentences!

I establish relationships between them.

I create harmony.

Before I tell you about my specific roles,
let me tell you about
PHRASES, CLAUSES and SENTENCES!

A PHRASE:
A group of words that
DOES NOT HAVE A SUBJECT OR VERB

"with a smile on her face"

A CLAUSE:
A group of words that
DOES HAVE A SUBJECT AND VERB

"I am studying Astronomy."

So, what kind of CLAUSES are there?

INDEPENDENT CLAUSE	DEPENDENT CLAUSE
It can stand alone, and it forms a complete thought.	It cannot stand alone, and it does not form a complete thought.
"I went to Greece."	"When I was in Greece..."

A SENTENCE always conveys a complete thought!

It can be one or more INDEPENDENT CLAUSES	Or	It can be one or more INDEPENDENT CLAUSES + One or more DEPENDENT CLAUSES
"I went to Greece and had a great time."		"I had a great time when I was in Greece."

Now that you understand
PHRASES, CLAUSES and SENTENCES
let's look at the roles I can play!

I'm called COORDINATE when I connect elements of equal rank.
(words, phrases or clauses)

By adding...

"Dylan and Tyler
are brothers."

* I connect two Nouns.

By opposing
or contrasting...

"It was raining, but
I enjoyed walking home."

* I connect two independent clauses.

By separating or choosing...

"Having ice cream or having cake is always a dilemma."

* I connect two phrases.

By concluding or inferring...

"Today is Election Day; so, I need to vote!"

* I connect two independent clauses.

I'm called SUBORDINATE when
I connect minor elements to major ones.

By denoting...

REASON or CAUSE

"He stopped eating **because** he was full."

* I connect one independent clause and one dependent clause.

COMPARISON or DEGREE

"I like English **as much as** I like Math."

* I connect one independent clause and one dependent clause.

By denoting...

TIME

"I'll play **until** my mother calls me."

* I connect one independent clause and one dependent clause.

PURPOSE or RESULT

"I went to bed early **so that** I would get enough rest."

* I connect one independent clause and one dependent clause.

By denoting...

MANNER

"Would you please show me **how** to play chess?"

* I connect one independent clause and one dependent clause.

PLACE

"He picked us up **where** he dropped us off."

* I connect one independent clause and one dependent clause.

Would you say I'm the most loving of all the actors?

If you need help "connecting", call me!

Now, please get paper & pencil so you can write down your answers!

CONJUNCTION EXERCISE #1

Guess whether I am COORDINATE or SUBORDINATE in the following sentences.

---

1. My parents and I will travel to Japan as soon as I finish school. __________

2. By the time the game ended, it was dark. __________

3. Their team lost today, yet they're optimistic they'll win the championship. __________

4. We didn't go to the beach because it was raining. __________

5. Amanda and Alexander love going to school. __________

6. The children like to swim, so we joined a health club. __________

CONJUNCTION EXERCISE #2

Draw a circle around me if I am COORDINATE and a heart around me if I am SUBORDINATE.

but	since	once
so	because	or
in order that	unless	after
for	yet	as much as

CONJUNCTION EXERCISE #3

In the following sentences I'm subordinate. Guess what I denote. Circle the right answer.

1. We stayed at the beach until the sun set.

   a) cause b) time c) place

2. Giraffes are taller than elephants.

   a) manner b) comparison c) cause

3. In sewing class I learned how to sew on a button.

   a) place b) manner c) result

4. Home is where the heart is.

   a) comparison b) cause c) place

5. I studied a lot so that I would get a good grade.

   a) comparison b) result c) cause

CONJUNCTION SUMMARY

I'm "The Great Matchmaker."
I connect words, phrases, clauses or sentences.

I'm called COORDINATE when I ADD, CONTRAST/OPPOSE, SEPARATE/CHOOSE, or CONCLUDE.

I'm called SUBORDINATE when I denote REASON/CAUSE, COMPARISON, CONDITION, MANNER, PLACE, TIME, or PURPOSE/RESULT.

And now, please, let's welcome our next awesome actor...

PREPOSITION

Hello! I'm PREPOSITION.

My name means "placed before"
because I come on stage before
NOUN, PRONOUN, ADJECTIVE, ADVERB
or even a whole sentence and I help
the sentence create a relationship with
any one of my fellow actors.

This can be very tricky.
That's why they call me "The Trickster."

In every play most of the special expressions are performed by me.

"I was accused by my brother of eating all the cookies."

Do you see how I changed the meaning of the word "accused"?

Do you know the difference between "accused by" and "accused of"?

Are you ready for some more fun tricks?

Sometimes only one of the parties
that I help connect is expressed.
The other you'll have to guess.

"Here is the car we came in." (vs.) "Here is the car in which we came."

And here are my "ON" tricks!

"Why are my boots on the refrigerator?"

"He talked on sharks."

"She paid on receiving the bill."

And here are a few more tricks.
Sometimes I play the role of ADJECTIVE or ADVERB.

"I'm a bird of great beauty!"

"She forgot her ballet shoes; she'll have to do without."

I can be SIMPLE.*

(a monosyllabic word)

"He is at the gym."

I can be DERIVED.*

(a word with two or more syllables or made of two or more words)

"We raced around the house."

*Some common SIMPLE PREPOSITIONS are:

at, as, by, for, from, in, on, of, off, to, up, and with

*Some common DERIVED PREPOSITIONS are:

about, above, across, after, along, around, before, below, except, inside, into, outside, onto, over, within, and without

I'm called PARTICIPIAL
when I force a participle to play my role.

"We will travel by boat
notwithstanding unfavorable weather."

*A PARTICIPLE is a VERBAL ADJECTIVE,
meaning an ADJECTIVE formed from a VERB. (e.g.: standing)

I'm called PHRASAL or a UNIT PREPOSITION when I'm made of two or more words.

"She swam in spite of her injury."

I'm called VERBAL when I'm inseparable from VERB.

With INFINITIVE I always wear my "TO" costume.

"I stand for peace."

"I like to cook."

*INFINITIVE is the root form of the verb that indicates infinite action without the limits of person or number (e.g. TO PLAY, TO WALK, TO SEE).

Now, please get paper & pencil so you can write down your answers!

PREPOSITION EXERCISE #1

Can you spot me on this page?
Draw a circle around me when you do!

---

from ah! at

love smart

inside for important

the books

lively tricky creating

by we

boasting music above

PREPOSITION EXERCISE #2

Guess if I'm simple or derived in the following sentences.

		simple	or	derived
1.	This is a gift for you.	☐		☐
2.	The waves splashed above her head.	☐		☐
3.	She walked across the park in the snow.	☐		☐
4.	Go along Main Street and turn left.	☐		☐
5.	I'll meet you at the movies.	☐		☐
6.	My books are already inside my bag.	☐		☐

PREPOSITION EXERCISE #3

Write three sentences using my "on" tricks.
Then draw a picture of one of them.

1.

2.

3.

PREPOSITION SUMMARY

My name means placed before.

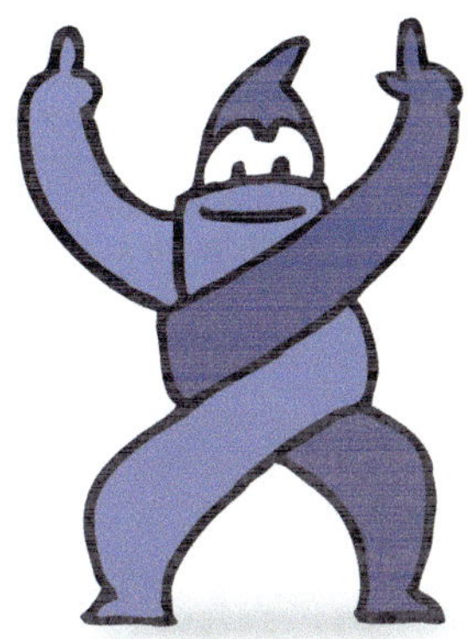

I come on stage before NOUN, PRONOUN, ADJECTIVE, ADVERB or a WHOLE SENTENCE and help it create a relationship with any of my fellow actors.

I can be SIMPLE or DERIVED.

I'm called PHRASAL when I'm made of two or more words.

I'm called VERBAL when I'm inseparable from verb.

I'm called PARTICIPIAL when I force a participle to play my role.

Sometimes I play the role of ADJECTIVE or ADVERB.

And now, please, let's welcome our next fabulous actor...

INTERJECTION

Hello! I'm INTERJECTION.

I never play with the others.
I work by myself and very independently.
I throw myself on the stage whenever I feel like it.
I express strong or sudden feelings.

An exclamation point often pops up right next to me.

I can express:

attention "Look!"

dislike "Ugh!"

calling "Hello!"

departure "Goodbye!"

excitement "Hurray!"

interrogation "Hmm. Really!"

joy "Wheeee!"

laughter "Ha-ha!"

pain	"Ouch!"
praise	"Great!"
salutation	"Greetings!"
silencing	"Shhh! Quiet!"
relief	"Whew!"
surprise	"Wow!"
wonder	"Whoa!"

...and many more!!!

I really can express every feeling that exists.

Hmm...
should I have a flexibility contest with Adjective???

Now, please get paper & pencil so you can write down your answers!

INTERJECTION EXERCISE #1

Guess the feeling I express in each of the words below.

1. Cheers! ______
2. Excellent! ______
3. Shhhhhh! ______
4. Darn! ______
5. Yuck! ______
6. Yes! ______
7. Oops! ______
8. Hurrah! ______
9. Boo! ______
10. Eureka! ______
11. Thanks! ______
12. Bravo! ______
13. Really? ______
14. Whew! ______
15. Holy cow! ______

INTERJECTION EXERCISE #2

Draw a picture related to one of the feelings on the opposite page.

INTERJECTION SUMMARY

I NEVER play with the others.

I always express strong or sudden feelings like:

Joy

Surprise

Attention

Question

Dislike

Praise

Laughter

Wonder

.... and many more just like these!

An exclamation point often pops up next to me!

Believe it or not, it's the end of this show....
but before we go, come out actors and take a bow!!!

ADVERB
I perform with VERB.
ADJECTIVE
I enhance NOUN and PRONOUN.
VERB
I am action itself.
NOUN
I name.
PRONOUN
I replace NOUN.

Thank you for coming to the show!
INTERJECTION
I show strong emotions!!!
CONJUNCTION
I connect.
PREPOSITION
I create relationships.
ARTICLE
I point to NOUN.
Now go create your own play!

Now you can check your answers on the following pages.

EXERCISE ANSWERS VERB

VERB EXERCISE #1

1. order
2. active
3. fact
4. event
5. passive
6. adjective
7. noun
8. subjunctive

VERB EXERCISE #2

(This picture will be unique to each Student.)

VERB EXERCISE #3

1. Question
2. Possibility
3. Purpose
4. Question
5. Necessity
6. Obligation

EXERCISE ANSWERS
NOUN

NOUN EXERCISE #1

1. Object
2. Subject
3. Object
4. Object
5. Subject
6. Object
7. Subject
8. Subject
9. Subject

NOUN EXERCISE #2

1. Singular
2. Plural
3. Singular
4. Singular
5. Plural
6. Singular
7. Plural
8. Singular
9. Plural
10. Plural
11. Singular
12. Singular or Plural

NOUN EXERCISE #3

- Bear
- Italy
- apple
- courage
- boat
- orchestra
- piglets
- Jason
- violin
- height
- trees
- Kitchen
- eyes
- horse
- paper

EXERCISE ANSWERS
ARTICLE

ARTICLE EXERCISE #1

1. Definite
2. Indefinite
3. Indefinite - Definite
4. Indefinite
5. Indefinite - Definite
6. Indefinite - Definite

ARTICLE EXERCISE #2

Yesterday, I went to the zoo with my father. I saw a lion and his cubs, a hippopotamus, an elephant, many deer, many tigers and a chimpanzee. All the animals seemed well-cared for and happy.

ARTICLE EXERCISE #3

(This picture will be unique to each Student.)

EXERCISE ANSWERS
ADVERB

ADVERB EXERCISE #1

It means: "Near the VERB."

ADVERB EXERCISE #2

1. degree
2. time
3. place
4. reason
5. negation
6. verbal
7. interrogative

ADVERB EXERCISE #3

(This picture will be unique to each Student.)

EXERCISE ANSWERS ADJECTIVE

ADJECTIVE EXERCISE #1

1. Thankful
2. Greenish
3. Effortless
4. Floral
5. Sailing
6. Cooperative
7. Courageous
8. Encouraged
9. Interactive
10. Extraordinary
11. Subordinate
12. Eastern

ADJECTIVE EXERCISE #2

1. Pure
2. Proper
3. Derived
4. Poetical
5. Pronominal
6. Substantive

ADJECTIVE EXERCISE #3

1. More
2. More
3. Less
4. More
5. More
6. Less

EXERCISE ANSWERS
PRONOUN

PRONOUN EXERCISE #1

It means: "In place of the NOUN."

PRONOUN EXERCISE #2

1. I love you.
   Personal / Personal

2. Our teacher told us to be quiet.
   Possessive / Personal

3. The Grammar Book is mine.
   Possessive

4. The poem that he wrote about friendship was beautiful.
   Relative /Personal

5. His puppy barked at us.
   Possessive / Personal

6. Who do you think is stronger?
   Interrogative / Personal

7. We painted our home ourselves.
   Personal / Possessive / Reflexive

EXERCISE ANSWERS
CONJUNCTION

CONJUNCTION EXERCISE #1

1. Subordinate
2. Subordinate
3. Coordinate
4. Subordinate
5. Coordinate
6. Coordinate

CONJUNCTION EXERCISE #3

1. Time
2. Comparison
3. Manner
4. Place
5. Result

CONJUNCTION EXERCISE #2

But	〉	circle
Since	〉	heart
Once	〉	heart
Yet	〉	circle
Because	〉	heart
Or	〉	circle
So	〉	circle
In order that	〉	heart
Unless	〉	heart
After	〉	heart
For	〉	circle
As much as	〉	heart

EXERCISE ANSWERS PREPOSITION

PREPOSITION EXERCISE #1

- From
- At
- Inside
- For
- By
- Above

PREPOSITION EXERCISE #2

1. Simple
2. Derived
3. Derived
4. Derived
5. Simple
6. Derived

PREPOSITION EXERCISE #3

(This drawing will be unique to each Student.)

EXERCISE ANSWERS INTERJECTION

INTERJECTION EXERCISE #1

1.	Cheers!	›	Salutation
2.	Excellent!	›	Praise
3.	Shhhhhh!	›	Silencing
4.	Darn!	›	Frustration
5.	Yuck!	›	Disgust
6.	Yes!	›	Satisfaction, approval
7.	Oops!	›	Mistake
8.	Hurrah!	›	Happiness, triumph
9.	Boo!	›	Surprise, scare
10.	Eureka!	›	Discovery, surprise
11.	Thanks!	›	Appreciation
12.	Bravo!	›	Praise
13.	Really?	›	Surprise, disbelief
14.	Whew!	›	Relief
15.	Holy cow!	›	Surprise, astonishment

INTERJECTION EXERCISE #2

(This drawing will be unique to each Student.)